People of Destiny

A Humanities Series

There comes a time,
we know not when,
that marks
the destiny of men.

Joseph Addison Alexander

People of Destiny

JOHN F. KENNEDY

By John P. Reidy and Norman Richards

CHILDRENS PRESS, CHICAGO

*The editors wish to express
their appreciation to Mr. Meyer Goldberg,
who created the series and inspired
the publication of* People of Destiny.

Cover and body design: John Hollis

Project editor: Joan Downing

Editorial assistant: Gerri Stoller

---

*Illustrations: Bob Brunton—Hollis
Associates*

Research editor: Robert Hendrickson

---

*Photographs: From the files of Wide World
Photos, Inc.*

Typesetting: American Typesetting Co.

Printing: The Regensteiner Corporation

*Quotations on pages 43, 44, and 50 from PT 109—John Kennedy
in World War II, by Robert J. Donavan. Copyright 1961 by
McGraw-Hill Book Company. Used by permission of McGraw-
Hill Book Company.*
*Quotation on page 73 from Kennedy, by Theodore Sorenson.
Published by Harper & Row, 1965.*

4 5 6 7 8 9 10 11 12 13 14 15 16 17 18 19 20 21 22 23 24 25 R 75 74 73 72 71 70

Contents

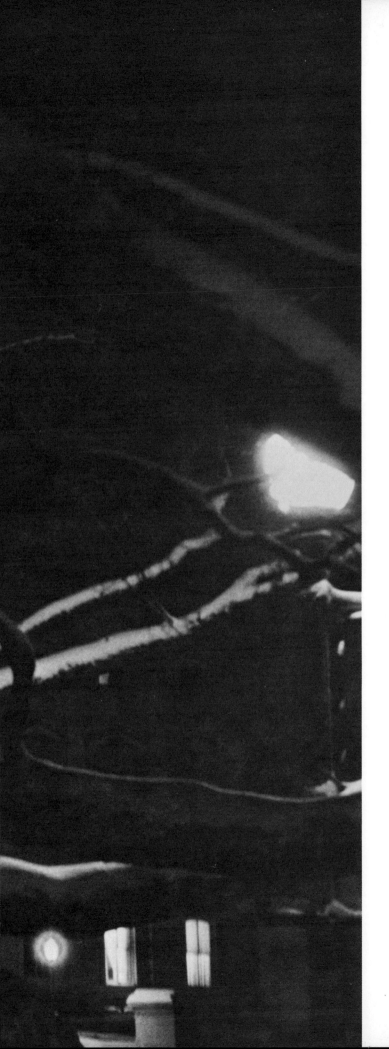

The Passing of the Torch

On the morning of January 20, 1961, the city of Washington, D.C. crackled with excitement, as it always does on Inauguration Day. People from all over the country had come to watch the giant parade and the ceremonies surrounding the swearing in of a new president. Millions more were planning to watch the proceedings on television. People talked excitedly about the man who was about to become the thirty-fifth President of the United States: John Fitzgerald Kennedy.

A fierce snowstorm had raged the previous day and night, threatening to mar the occasion, but the city awoke to find a brilliant sun shining on eight inches of snow. It was bitterly cold, however, and the workmen's breath was visible in the frosty air as they labored to complete the platform in front of the Capitol Building.

Across the street from the White House a crowd gathered to watch the arrival of government officials. People

bundled in overshoes, heavy coats, and gloves, stood in the snow watching the cars pull into the White House driveway. At about eleven o'clock that morning the black presidential limousine turned slowly through the gates and the crowd murmured excitedly. It stopped at the White House portico and the youthful, vigorous President-elect stepped out with his lovely wife, Jacqueline. The outgoing President, Dwight D. Eisenhower, greeted them warmly.

A half hour later the two men walked outside wearing top hats and posed for pictures as the crowd cheered. They were soon joined by the outgoing Vice-President, Richard Nixon, and the newly elected Vice-President, Lyndon Johnson, with their wives and several Congressional leaders. The group entered a line of waiting automobiles, with Eisenhower and Kennedy in the first car. The presidential procession moved slowly down Pennsylvania Avenue.

A tremendous crowd of people greeted them when they reached the Capitol and stepped onto the ceremonial platform. Former President Harry S. Truman was among the dignitaries who joined them on the platform in the biting cold wind. The ceremonies opened with the singing of the National Anthem. Richard Cardinal Cushing of Boston, a close friend of the Kennedy family, then gave the invocation. Prayers were offered by representatives of the major religions and one of America's most famous poets, Robert Frost, recited a poem he had composed for the occasion.

Then the most important moment arrived. Earl Warren, Chief Justice of the Supreme Court, administered the oath of office. John F. Kennedy placed his hand on an old family Bible and solemnly pledged himself to uphold the duties of the presidency. He stood erect in the bitter cold without a topcoat or hat, the sun glinting on his chestnut-colored hair.

The oath completed, the new President turned to face "his" people. His Inaugural Address, delivered with simplicity, seemed to be directed to the youth of America and the world. John F. Kennedy—concerned with the spirit of America—spoke:

"We observe today," he said, "not a victory of party but a celebration of freedom, symbolizing an end as well as a beginning, signifying renewal as well as change. For I have sworn before you and Almighty God the same oath our forebears prescribed nearly a century and three quarters ago.

"The world is very different now. For man holds in his mortal hands the power to abolish all forms of human life. And yet the same revolutionary beliefs for which our forefathers fought are still at issue around the globe—the belief that the rights of man come not from the generosity of the state but from the hand of God.

On January 20, 1961, President of the United States John F. Kennedy was inaugurated. Here, President Kennedy and his wife sit in the rear seat of an open car as his inauguration parade makes it way down Constitution Avenue enroute to the White House in Washington (opposite top). The Capitol is in the background. Opposite, bottom: Spectators crowd in front of the inauguration stand as President Kennedy takes his oath of office, administered by Chief Justice Earl Warren.

*"...ask not what your country
can do for you; ask what
you can do for your country..."*

"We dare not forget today that we are the heirs of that first revolution. . . ."

He went on to describe some of America's aims and ideals: close co-operation with our allies, a new "alliance for progress" to help the countries of Latin America, support for the United Nations, and help for the poor and unfortunate people all over the world.

He spoke with youthful fervor and idealism, and the audience listened intently—especially the young people.

Stabbing the air with his forefinger to emphasize the point, he declared, ". . . Let the word go forth from this time and place, to friend and foe alike, that the torch has been passed to a new generation of Americans, born in this century, tempered by war, disciplined by a hard and bitter peace, proud of our ancient heritage, and unwilling to witness or permit the slow undoing of those human rights to which this nation has always been committed, and to which we are committed today at home and around the world. . . ."

Speaking for the new generation, he said, ". . . In the long history of the world, only a few generations have been granted the role of defending freedom in its hour of maximum danger. I do not shrink from this responsibility; I wel-

come it. I do not believe that any of us would exchange places with any other people or any other generation. The energy, the faith, the devotion which we bring to this endeavor will light our country and all who serve it, and the glow from that fire can truly light the world.

"And so, my fellow Americans, ask not what your country can do for you; ask what you can do for your country.

"My fellow citizens of the world, ask not what America will do for you, but what together we can do for the freedom of man. . . ."

When he finished, the young President received a tremendous ovation from the chilly throng. In one short speech John F. Kennedy had caught the imagination of the American people and the people of the world. He seemed to promise freshness and enthusiasm, as if he knew his destiny would be to inspire people the world over to strive toward the ideals of man with renewed energy.

He could not know how prominent that destiny would be. But millions of Americans came to realize that the torch had indeed been passed to a remarkable man whose name would live forever in his country's history.

After his inaugural address, President Kennedy watches the units marching by the reviewing stand during the inaugural parade.

The Boston Irish

John F. Kennedy's family roots go back to the green fields of Ireland, and they are linked with struggle and poverty. Ireland had always been a poor country beset by political troubles, but things were especially bad in the 1840's. Most Irishmen were farmers who rented small plots of land from landlords who lived in England. Rents were high and they had little money left with which to buy the necessities of life. Families lived in huts with dirt floors; their main food consisted of the potatoes they grew.

Tragedy struck the Irish farmers in 1845 and 1846. A blight killed nearly all the potato crops in the country, robbing many people of their only means of survival. Families wandered along the roads, hoping in vain to find in the fields a few potatoes that had not been hit by the blight. Thousands of people starved to death, and many more died of typhus disease, which spread at the time of the famine.

All hope seemed lost. Many Irishmen saw no other choice but to leave their stricken country. Some went to England, the strong, industrial country that controlled Ireland. Life in England was not easy for them, but they could find factory jobs that enabled them to earn enough to eat regularly.

Others had a dream of crossing the ocean to America, the "land of oppor-tunity." The young country was growing fast and becoming strong. American industry was becoming one of the most advanced in the world. Textile mills, furniture, cutlery, and machinery factories abounded in the older, better-established states in the East. Gold was discovered in California and thousands of people moved westward, battling Indians along the way. Soon cattle ranchers moved onto the open plains of the West and railroads were built across the continent, binding the young country together.

There was room for newcomers in such a country, and thousands of Irishmen sold all their belongings to scrape together enough money for passage across the ocean. Many of them headed westward to work as construction laborers on the railroads, while others settled in the older, larger cities in the East.

Patrick Kennedy, a youth from the town of New Ross in southeast Ireland, was one of the many who made his way to Boston. He spent every penny he had to buy a ticket on a ship to America. He rode steerage class, jammed uncomfortably with other emigrants in the cramped quarters. Because Boston was closer than any other American seaport and the fare was less, it attracted many of the Irish.

In 1845 and 1846, tragedy struck the Irish farmers. A blight killed nearly all the potato crops in the country, robbing many people of their only means of survival. Many Irishmen saw no other choice but to leave their stricken country. Patrick Kennedy, John F. Kennedy's great-grandfather, was one of the many who made his way to Boston. He rode steerage class on a ship much like the one at left, jammed uncomfortably with other emigrants in the cramped quarters.

Delighted at the opportunity for a fresh start, Patrick Kennedy didn't move far from the dock where he landed, but found work immediately as a cooper, or barrel maker. He settled in a crowded section known as East Boston, on the edge of busy Boston Harbor. Thousands of other recent Irish immigrants clung together in this area, living in cramped tenement houses, cellars, and attics. Most of them found jobs as unskilled laborers, but pay was low for this type of work and they had to struggle to make ends meet.

Besides being a busy seaport, Boston was at its peak as the literary and cultural center of America in 1850, when Patrick Kennedy arrived. Authors and poets such as Henry Wadsworth Longfellow, Nathaniel Hawthorne, Ralph Waldo Emerson, Henry Thoreau, and John Greenleaf Whittier made Boston their headquarters and spread its name to many parts of the world. At times called the "Athens of America" and the "Hub of the Universe," Boston was an intellectual capital for philosophers, musicians, artists, and leaders in education and medicine.

It was also the place where Donald McKay built many of the graceful clipper ships that broke speed records and made Boston seamen and merchants known around the world. Ship captains and owners made fortunes in the Far East trade, and whaling ships out of nearby New Bedford and Nan-

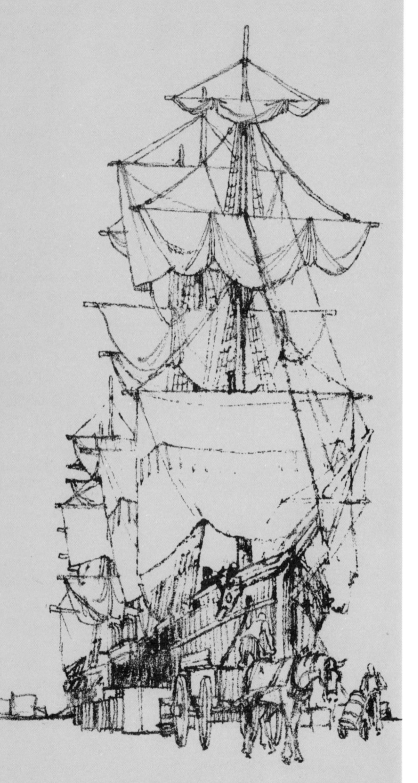

Patrick Kennedy found work as a cooper, or barrel maker. He married a young Irish girl and they had four children. Their only son, Patrick, Jr., went to work on the docks (above) as soon as he was old enough. His father had died shortly before the Civil War began in the United States.

tucket ranged over the globe to supply whale oil, the fuel used in most of America's lamps.

But Patrick Kennedy and other uneducated Irish immigrants had little chance to share in Boston's prosperity and achievement. The city was an orderly, settled community with few major problems. Most of the inhabitants were Protestant, Anglo-Saxon descendents of the original Puritan settlers. The city was not prepared for the sudden mass influx of Irish, and adequate housing was not available.

The unskilled Irish farmers, who had to take menial jobs and live in slums, were regarded by native Bostonians as "lower class," "crude," and "undesirable" as fellow workers and friends. Their "foreign" religion, Roman Catholicism, was thought to be something strange and secret.

Patrick Kennedy married a young Irish girl and soon they had three daughters and a son, Patrick, Jr. The father did not live to see his children grow up. He died shortly before the Civil War began in the United States, and his widow was left to support her children.

Patrick, Jr. went to work on the docks as soon as he was old enough, and before he was twenty he decided there would be more money in owning a business than there was in working for wages. He borrowed and saved enough money to make a down pay-

ment on a saloon where his fellow dock workers invariably stopped and spent part of their pay. He managed it shrewdly, and soon he had enough money to buy several more saloons. In a few years he was able to buy into a coal business and became one of the most prosperous residents of the East Boston Irish community. He was a quiet, cautious young man who earned the respect of all who knew him.

Patrick married Mary Hickey, a girl from another Irish family that had risen from the depths of poverty to a respectable position. In 1888 they had a son named Joseph Patrick. Patrick liked politics and soon became influential in local Democratic party wards. He served as fire commissioner, street commissioner, and election commissioner while continuing his successful businesses.

He was able to send his red-haired son to Harvard, and young Joe worked hard in his spare time and earned a considerable amount of money. He had inherited his father's business ability, but little did anyone realize how successful this young man would become.

While the taciturn, hard-working Patrick Kennedy had been rising successfully in life, another Irishman named John F. Fitzgerald had been doing the same. A short, bouncy, witty politician, he had started at the bottom and became a councilman, an alderman, a state legislator, a United States Congressman and, finally, mayor of Boston. He always sang his favorite song, "Sweet Adeline," for crowds when he campaigned for election. He came to be known as "Honey Fitz."

Patrick, Jr. had borrowed and saved enough money by the time he was twenty to make a down payment on a saloon. He soon married and had a son, Joseph Patrick. While Patrick Kennedy had been rising successfully in life, another Irishman named John F. Fitzgerald had been doing the same. Fitzgerald, known as "Honey Fitz," was a politician who eventually became mayor of Boston. He is shown at left in a 1910 picture with his lovely daughter, Rose.

Fitzgerald and Kennedy knew each other, of course, since both were involved in politics, but both were surprised to find that young Joe Kennedy was courting Fitzgerald's lovely daughter, Rose. Joe was a worthy suitor, indeed. Using some of his father's money, he had managed to gain control of a faltering East Boston bank, the Columbia Trust Company. He was a bank president at the age of twenty-five, and he managed the bank so skillfully that it began to show a profit. He declared to Rose that he would make himself a millionaire by the time he was thirty-five.

The young couple were married in the private chapel of the Archbishop of Boston in October, 1914. It was a time of tension in the world, for the major European nations were at war in the beginning of a struggle that would later be known as World War I. Germany and Austria were battling Great Britain, France, Russia, and several other nations; the powerful German armies were menacing France, the Netherlands, and Belgium. Not long afterward, the Germans drove toward Paris and the French and British troops defended France in terrible, bloody battles. After attacks by German submarines on American ships, the United States declared war on Germany in 1917. Soon a million American troops and millions of tons of supplies were being shipped overseas.

Joe Kennedy became assistant general manager of Bethlehem Steel's huge shipyards at Quincy, near Boston, and did a remarkable job of administrating. But when the war ended in 1918 with America and her allies victorious, he wanted to change his work and go into the business of high finance. Through his shipyard business experience he had met one of Wall Street's biggest financiers, Galen Stone, who was the owner of the Boston investment firm of Hayden, Stone. Stone was so impressed by the intelligence and ambition of young Joe Kennedy that he gave him a job as head of his stock department.

It was the perfect opportunity to learn the world of finance, and Joe lost no time in taking advantage of it. Soon he was making his own investment deals in his spare time, and he invested so wisely that he began to make large profits. Within a few years he was making so much money that he was able to resign at Hayden, Stone and devote full time to his investments. He bought into motion picture companies, theaters, and many other industries and sold out at huge profits. Later, he was to escape the stock market crash of 1929 by selling his stocks before the crash. Instead of the bankruptcy that was the fate of so many investors, Joseph Kennedy had a huge fortune in cash.

Driven by ambition and possessed of brilliant business ability, Joe Kennedy reached his goal of being a millionaire by the time he was thirty-five. In fact, he was a millionaire several times over, and this fortune was to play a decisive role in the lives of his children.

Patrick Kennedy liked politics and had become influential in local Democratic party wards. He served as fire commissioner, street commissioner, and election commissioner while continuing his successful business. Because they were both involved in politics, Kennedy and Fitzgerald knew each other, but both were surprised to find that young Joe Kennedy was courting Fitzgerald's daughter, Rose. Joe had used some of his father's money to gain control of a faltering East Boston bank, and had become bank president at the age of twenty-five. The young couple were married in October, 1914. They are shown at left on their wedding day.

Second Best

Joe Kennedy settled down with his lovely bride in a large, rambling, gray house in Brookline, a middle class suburb of Boston. Within a year she gave birth to a boy, whom they proudly named Joseph P. Kennedy, Jr. On May 29, 1917, they had a second son, whom they named John Fitzgerald Kennedy, after his maternal grandfather, "Honey Fitz." Over the years the family grew to be a large one, with four sons and five daughters. The two youngest were Robert and Edward.

Impulsive, impatient, hot-tempered Joe Kennedy proved to be a loving father to his children. He was stern, however, and he encouraged self-reliance and ambition. He stressed competitiveness as a virtue and lectured to them over and over again on the importance of winning. As busy as he was with his travels and business dealings, he spent every possible hour he could with his children.

Joe Kennedy's roughness was countered by the gentleness and spiritual inspiration of his wife, who was the real backbone of the family. Years later her children credited Rose Kennedy with being the strength that helped them all in times of tragedy or worry.

Joe, Jr. was just about everything a proud father could ask for; he was the apple of his father's eye. He was friendly, outgoing, good at athletics, and a student who brought home excellent grades.

In contrast, his younger brother John, or Jack, as he was called, was shy, introverted, and a lover of books. He was of slighter build than Joe and always came out second best when they fought or competed in games. Like many an older brother, Joe delighted in fighting with Jack and winning. Jack fought stubbornly and they had some fierce battles as they were growing up. Both boys began their schooling at Dexter Academy, a private school a few blocks from home. Joe got top grades, while Jack's were mediocre at best. Their father always compared their grades and berated Jack for not doing as well as Joe. The youngster, who showed little interest in schoolwork, dreaded being compared with his older brother.

Besides encouraging his children to compete in sports, Joe Kennedy developed the practice of discussing American government and world events with them at the dinner table. They were expected to be aware of and express opinions about current events. Many a lively debate was carried on as they became older.

By the time Jack entered the fourth grade, the family had moved to a suburb of New York City, so that Joseph Kennedy could be closer to his Wall Street investment dealings. By the time Jack had completed the sixth grade, Joe, Jr. was enrolled at Choate Academy in Connecticut, an exclusive private school affiliated with the Episcopalian faith. Rose Kennedy wanted Jack to have some training at a Catholic school, since he had not had much

Joe and Rose Kennedy had nine children. Both Joe, Jr., the oldest, and his younger brother Jack began their schooling at Dexter Academy, a private school a few blocks from their home in Brookline, Massachusetts. Opposite, Jack is shown as he appeared in a football uniform of Dexter School, about 1927.

religious training at his previous schools, so he was enrolled at the Canterbury School in Connecticut.

It was Jack's first experience in living away from his warm family environment, and he was homesick at first. He had trouble with Latin and his overall grades were only moderately good, but he showed good grades in English and history. Like many a thoughtful boy who loves books, he was absentminded about daily practical things.

An attack of appendicitis cut short his year at Canterbury. Jack went home to recuperate after the operation.

The next fall Jack followed his father's wishes and enrolled at Choate, which meant he again would be in competition with Joe, Jr. His older brother was a top all-around student, who not only was on the honor roll but also was one of the school's best athletes and most-popular students.

Jack never attained that status, although he did play intramural sports and was popular with the other students. In fact, his room became something of a clubhouse for them.

Again, Latin was his worst subject, but he continued to be a top student in the courses he liked. His English instructor, Harold Tinker, told him:

"Your penmanship could certainly take a bit of improving but you've got a gift in your pen. I think you've got the gift of a writer in you if you ever take it seriously enough."

It wasn't until his senior year at Choate that Jack began to think seriously about his future. He finally realized that the only way to succeed is by hard work.

He did improve his grades in his senior year, and that summer, following graduation, he attended the London School of Economics, as Joe, Jr. had done previously. By fall he seemed ready to do a good job in college, but illness delayed him and he started late.

Joe, Jr. had gone on to Harvard, his father's alma mater, and was continuing to distinguish himself as a student, athlete, and popular young man. Jack had been expected to follow his older brother to Harvard, but he decided to go to Princeton instead, where his Choate roommates, Rip Horton and Lem Billings, were going. His father may have been disappointed, but he believed his children should be encouraged to make their own decisions, and he agreed to it.

When he seemed cured of the jaundice that he had contracted that summer, Jack entered Princeton and tried to catch up to his classmates. But the illness struck again two months later and he had to withdraw from the school. His parents sent him to Arizona for most of the winter to regain his health.

It was a disappointed and somewhat anxious young Jack Kennedy who was forced to wait until the following autumn to begin college. This time he chose the path that made his father happy. Rather than enter Princeton a year behind his old Choate friends, he enrolled as a freshman at Harvard.

The Joseph Kennedy family is shown in the picture on the opposite page as they appeared after an audience with Pope Pius XII in 1939. By this time, Joseph Kennedy had been appointed Ambassador to Great Britain by President Franklin Delano Roosevelt. The only member of the family missing from this picture is Joe, Jr.

A Harvard Student Grows Up

Joseph Kennedy had bought a large, rambling summer home at Hyannis Port on Cape Cod, Massachusetts. This became the center of the Kennedy family—the place where they gathered, no matter where the members might be scattered in the years to come. It was a lovely old New England house with a large porch overlooking the beach and Nantucket Sound. The Kennedy children spent all their summers here, swimming, sailing, playing softball and touch football. The girls, led by Kathleen, the oldest and closest to Jack, played as competitively as the boys did in these games.

Jack and the others grew up loving the sea, the wind, the smell of the salt air, the sound of crashing surf on the beach. They were all adept at sailing, and the Kennedy name was a familiar one when the winners of local boat races were announced.

Joseph Kennedy, who had continued his interest in politics, gave financial support to an old acquaintance, Franklin Delano Roosevelt, when the New York governor ran for president in 1932. The country was in a terrible economic depression that year and many factories were idle and the workers out of jobs. So many people were poverty-stricken that the feeling was that something drastic had to be done. The Democratic party candidate, Roosevelt, promised relief to the unemployed workers in a variety of ways. He was elected in 1932, and immediately began taking measures to help the country out of the depression.

As a freshman at Harvard, Jack discovered the same old comparisons with Joe, Jr., who had grown to be a tall, handsome young man who played varsity football and won elections to many posts in extracurricular organizations. Jack went out for football, swimming, golf, and softball, but he was too slight to do well, even though he tried with fierce determination.

The Kennedy children spent all their summers at a large, rambling summer home at Hyannis Port on Cape Cod, Massachusetts, that Joseph Kennedy had bought. They swam, sailed, played softball and touch football, and grew up loving the sea, the wind, the smell of the salt air, and the sound of crashing surf. All were adept at sailing and won many local boat races.

During the summer after his freshman year at Harvard, Jack Kennedy toured Europe with a friend. Adolf Hitler (left) had become head of the German government and was building a large army. Everywhere Jack went he saw in people fear of another war. As he traveled, Jack began to understand how international politics made history.

His best sport was swimming, but even here he had bad luck. He came down with a severe cold just before the trials were to be held to select members of the team that was to compete against Yale. Even worse, he was sent to the college infirmary for rest and recovery. Jack was desperate in his desire to make the team, and he persuaded a friend to smuggle steaks and milk shakes to him in the infirmary, to build up his strength. He still had a fever when the time came for the trials, but he dressed and went over to the pool building to take part in the trials. He poured every bit of his strength into his performance, but he lost his heat and failed to make the team. Once more he had to write home and say that he had failed at something that Joe would have found easy. But the seemingly unfair competition between these two very different brothers only served to toughen Jack's spirit and determination. Many years later he would remark that Joe's victories and inspiration had helped shape his own character.

Jack failed to make the varsity in football, but he played on the second-string freshman team, hoping to convince the coach that he had the sheer determination to qualify for the first team, even if he didn't have the natural ability. Here he ran into more bad luck. During a practice session he was tackled very hard and was slow in getting up from the frozen ground. His back pained him intensely, and a few days later he went to the university medical office to have it examined. The doctors told him it was more than a sprain, and was probably a spinal injury. He was instructed to avoid all contact sports and violent exercises until it had healed. It never did heal completely, and his college football hopes were ended.

During his freshman year, Jack's grades weren't as high as Joe's. He joined two clubs, however, and was spending much of his time working on the business staff of the college newspaper, the Harvard *Crimson*, and serving on several student committees.

When the school term ended, Jack was given a pleasant surprise by his father: he would be allowed to take a trip through Europe that summer with an old school chum from Choate. It was an exciting summer for Jack, who had never been on his own before. He and his friend wandered all over Europe, talking with people in all walks of life. His father had provided them with letters of introduction to diplomats and businessmen, so the boys were able to discuss the situation in Europe with some knowledgeable people.

Jack's eyes were opened to history in the making, for Europe was undergoing rapid changes. A power-hungry man named Adolf Hitler had become head of the German government and was busy building a large army. He was threatening the other European countries, demanding more living space for the German people. Everywhere Jack went he saw in people fear of another war. In Italy another dictator ruled the government, and he, too, was threatening to conquer other countries. This man, Benito Mussolini, and Hitler formed a partnership, which increased the concern of many Europeans. As he traveled, Jack began to understand world events and how international politics made history.

After he returned to Harvard that fall he received news that kindled his interest in world events still further. President Roosevelt had been reelected to office the year before, and he appointed Joseph Kennedy Ambassador to Great Britain. Jack's parents moved to London, where they lived in a mansion with his younger brothers and sisters. The older boys and girls stayed

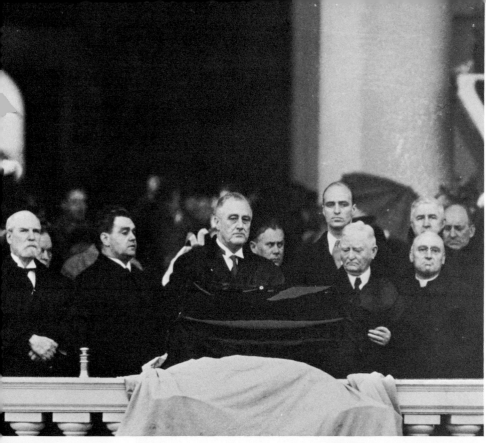

After Jack Kennedy returned
to Harvard for his sophomore
year, he received news that
kindled his interest in
world events still further.
President Roosevelt had been
reelected to office the year
before (left, top, at inauguration) and he appointed Joseph
Kennedy Ambassador to
Great Britain (left, bottom).
Jack's parents moved to
London with his younger
brothers and sisters. Europe
was still on the verge of war,
and though British Prime
Minister Neville Chamberlain
tried in 1938 to negotiate for
peace with Reichsführer
Adolf Hitler (opposite), the
negotiations failed.

at school in the United States. When Jack's sophomore year ended, he and Joe went to London to spend the summer with their parents.

Joe had graduated from Harvard and planned to attend Harvard Law School in the fall. He had decided on a career in politics, and fully intended to be President of the United States. His father had begun thinking seriously about the future possibility. Jack, on the other hand, knew he wasn't suited for politics, and furthermore, he didn't want to enter the field. Joe was obviously better suited.

Jack's grades improved considerably in his junior year, and he began to enjoy learning. He became fascinated with a course in American government, for he now could see how politics and governments affected the world in general. In 1939 he toured Europe again, this time with a serious purpose: he wanted to study the political situation and write reports on it.

Shortly after he completed his tour and returned to the American embassy in London, Hitler's army invaded Poland. The well-trained German soldiers quickly won battle after battle. It was clear that Poland would soon be conquered. At last Great Britain and France declared war on Germany.

Jack, now back at Harvard, was getting excellent grades. He began working hard on his senior thesis—a long report that would require much study and research. He chose to write about the situation in Europe as he had seen and studied it during the previous two years. He wanted to show that England and France had failed to discourage Hitler from demanding more territory by appeasing him, and that they had failed to prepare for war while the Germans built up their army. It seemed to him that these countries had been sleeping while Germany had been busy. Now they were too late to stop Hitler, who

had taken over the countries of Denmark, Norway, and the Netherlands as well as Poland, Austria, and Czechoslovakia. Jack declared in the thesis that the United States must build up its armed forces and avoid being unprepared if war should come. He spent long evenings in the college library gathering facts for his paper, and he studied everything he could find about the events that led up to the war. His hard work was rewarded; the university announced that his thesis had been accepted with highest honors.

Jack graduated in June, 1940, with honors in political science, and his parents were very proud. They couldn't come to the ceremony because of urgent duties in England, but Joseph Kennedy sent a wire to his son:

TWO THINGS I ALWAYS KNEW ABOUT YOU. ONE THAT YOU ARE SMART. TWO THAT YOU ARE A SWELL GUY. LOVE DAD.

Jack was so encouraged by Harvard's evaluation of his thesis that he decided he would like to try to have it published as a book. The manuscript, titled *Why England Slept*, was accepted by a publisher and quickly rushed into print, since the subject was very much in the news. France had surrendered to the invading German army and now England stood alone against Hitler's forces and was in deep trouble. The book promptly became a best seller, with forty thousand copies sold in the United States and another forty thousand in England. Jack was happy with his success as an author, but he still didn't know what he wanted to do in life. That fall he enrolled in the graduate school of business at Stanford University in California, but he dropped out after a short while, realizing that business was not the career for him.

Jack's father resigned as ambassador and came home to look after his vast

---

In 1939 Jack Kennedy toured Europe again, this time to study the political situation and write reports on it. Shortly after he completed his tour and returned to the American embassy in London, Hitler's army invaded Poland and soon Great Britain and France declared war on Germany. German air and ground troops are shown on page 32 at the time of the Polish invasion. John F. Kennedy's book, Why England Slept, *is an account of his observations of the events leading up to the war.*

business empire. It was becoming more and more apparent that the United States would become involved in the war. America had already sent supplies to help the British. When Joe, Jr. completed his second year of law school in June of 1941, he decided it wouldn't be long before war began for the United States. The Japanese had a military government much like Hitler's and were threatening countries in Asia. Their army had already invaded China and occupied much of the country, and they planned to conquer more of Asia. The United States warned Japan not to attempt any more aggression and the two countries were soon threatening each other.

Joe entered the naval aviation cadet-training program and soon won his wings as a navy pilot. Jack thought about doing the same thing, but decided to enter the Army Air Corps instead. He was told by the army doctors, however, that his injured back would prevent him from serving any military duty. Jack felt keenly disappointed, but by now he had become used to trying all the harder when he had failed. For the next five months he underwent treatments and exercises to strengthen his back muscles. Finally he tried for a commission as a naval officer and managed to pass the physical examination. At last he was in the service.

When Joe Kennedy, Jr. completed his second year of law school in June of 1941, he decided it wouldn't be long before war began for the United States. The French and English were fighting in Europe and needed United States help. French troops are shown arriving at a British port (opposite top) after heroically fighting their way out of Dunkirk. The Japanese military government was threatening countries in Asia. Their army had already invaded China (opposite bottom) and occupied much of the country, and they planned to conquer more of Asia. Joe entered the naval aviation cadet-training program and soon won his wings as a navy pilot (left).

Jack Kennedy was commissioned an ensign in the navy and was assigned to the Intelligence Division in Washington, D.C. On December 7, 1941, the Japanese attacked the American naval base at Pearl Harbor. Opposite top: Japanese newsreel picture showing Japanese fliers going to their planes aboard a carrier to start the raid on Pearl Harbor. Opposite bottom: Another Japanese newsreel picture shows Japanese aircraft carriers en route to attack Pearl Harbor. The drawing above depicts the American airfield at Pearl Harbor under attack by Japanese planes. The Japanese quickly followed up by invading the Philippines, Hong Kong, Malaya, and other places in Asia. The United States was in the war, and Jack Kennedy was tranferred to motor torpedo boat training.

After being commissioned an ensign, he was ordered to report to naval headquarters at Washington, D.C., where he was assigned to the Intelligence Division. As a junior officer his duties were not particularly interesting, and Jack was often restless in his desk job. His main duty was to prepare a daily news report for higher-ranking officers and he worked at it diligently. The armed forces were busily preparing for war and it certainly looked as if it were coming, but Jack didn't feel he was contributing much to the effort.

Then it happened: on December 7, 1941, the Japanese navy attacked the American naval base at Pearl Harbor, Hawaii, with airplanes launched from aircraft carriers at sea. The surprise attack was successful and several vital American warships were sunk—the very heart of the Pacific fleet. America had been dealt a staggering blow and the Japanese quickly followed up by invading the Philippines, Hong Kong, Malaya, and other places in Asia.

General Douglas MacArthur was commander of the small American and Filipino forces in the Philippines. Supplies were low and it was not possible to send more help for them, but MacArthur conducted a brilliant defense designed to slow the enemy advance. The battle raged fiercely for months.

Germany and Italy quickly declared war on the United States and now the Second World War had spread around the world. America began to convert its vast industries to making war supplies and drafted men to form a huge army, navy, marine corps, and coast guard. Those already in the armed forces were given additional training for combat duty when possible.

After several frustrating months, Jack was transferred to a type of duty he wanted: motor torpedo boat training. He was on his way to a date with destiny.

Combat In PT Boats

The motor torpedo boat, known as the PT boat, was one of the navy's smallest, fastest, and most useful craft. No bigger than many pleasure boats, it carried a crew of two officers and ten enlisted men. Its main function was to race in close to larger enemy ships, release torpedoes, and escape at full speed. It was also used to patrol islands and coastal areas because it was small and could be concealed easily. Its lightweight hull was made of flimsy plywood —scant protection against enemy firepower—but its three twelve-cylinder engines gave it such speed and maneuverability that it didn't have to stand and fight. It was capable of inflicting heavy damage with torpedo tubes that could be launched in an instant, and guns that could shoot down low-flying airplanes that swooped in to attack it. When General MacArthur had to escape from the Philippines to Australia, he did it in a PT boat. The Japanese captured the Philippines but couldn't capture MacArthur.

The navy discovered it had a ready-made group of capable captains for these boats, made up of hundreds of young college graduates from wealthy families. These young officers had grown up with sailboats and cabin cruisers. The excitement and dash of the PT boats appealed to them and they applied for training at the PT boat school in Mellville, Rhode Island.

Among them was Jack Kennedy, who had no difficulty with the eight-week course and felt pretty much at home operating boats in the same waters he had sailed as a youth. The course consisted of seamanship, navigation, engineering, torpedo handling, and gunnery. Jack's grades were excellent. His Harvard roommate, Torbert MacDonald, was with him in the school and he

The motor torpedo boat, known as the PT boat, was one of the navy's smallest, fastest, and most useful craft. It was capable of inflicting heavy damage to larger enemy ships and low-flying airplanes. Its main protection was its speed and maneuverability. When General Douglas MacArthur had to escape from the Philippines to Australia, he did it in a PT boat. The Japanese captured the Philippines but couldn't capture MacArthur. He is shown opposite at the time of his arrival in Australia.

became a close friend of two other young officers, Ensign Paul Fay and Ensign George Ross, who visited the Kennedy family at their home in Hyannis Port on weekends.

It was an enjoyable period, but each of the young men looked forward to serving overseas upon graduation. Jack had done so well, however, that he was assigned to the school as an instructor and promoted to lieutenant junior grade. He wanted combat duty, though, and requested a transfer, which finally came through in March of 1943, when he received his orders for duty in the Pacific.

After a long journey on two navy vessels, Lieutenant John F. Kennedy arrived at the PT boat base at Tulagi, near Guadalcanal in the Solomon Islands. The American forces and their allies were struggling to carry through an offensive against the Japanese. They had captured Guadalcanal after bloody fighting, and the entire offensive was centered in the Solomon chain. General MacArthur planned to capture island after island in the southwest Pacific, including the Philippines, until American forces were close enough to Japan to invade it. The Solomons were the first big step.

The base was little more than a group of huts clustered around some docks where the PT boats were tied up. It was on the edge of an oppressively hot, jungle-covered island. The PT boats would go out on missions from this base and return a short while later, since their fuel and range were limited.

Jack was assigned command of a dirty, worn-looking boat numbered 109 that had already seen nine months of combat duty. Its skipper was being transferred, but the executive officer, who was second in command, stayed with the boat. Jack was thankful for this, because the man was experienced. He was a huge former football player from Ohio named Leonard Thom. Jack had to pick the rest of his crew from among newly arrived men with as little combat experience as himself.

The men of the crew soon learned to like their new skipper, who didn't believe in formality. He wore the standard uniform of the wartime Pacific: khaki pants or shorts, no shirt, and a baseball cap. He spent most of his free time with his men and they became a close-knit group.

The crew hadn't been patrolling together long when orders came through for PT 109 and other boats to transfer to a new base at Rendova, 210 miles away. The Japanese navy was shipping supplies to its stranded troops on a number of islands, slipping past American air defenses under cover of darkness. Night after night destroyers sailed quietly through a stretch of water known as the Blackett Strait and unloaded supplies for their troops. The task of the PT boat squadron at Rendova was to patrol Blackett Strait nightly, attacking the enemy ships and shutting off the supplies. If they succeeded, the Americans would gain control of all the Solomon Islands. Without supplies the Japanese troops would have to surrender.

PT 109 and the other boats went out on patrol every night. For the first

In March of 1943, Lieutenant John F. Kennedy received his orders for duty in the Pacific. He was sent to the PT boat base at Tulagi, near Guadalcanal in the Solomon Islands, where he was assigned command of a dirty, worn-looking boat numbered 109. The American forces and their allies were carrying on an offensive against the Japanese. After being attacked by American airplanes during daylight hours (opposite), the Japanese navy was shipping supplies to its stranded troops on a number of islands under cover of darkness. The task of the PT boats was to patrol the area, attacking the enemy ships and shutting off the supplies.

40

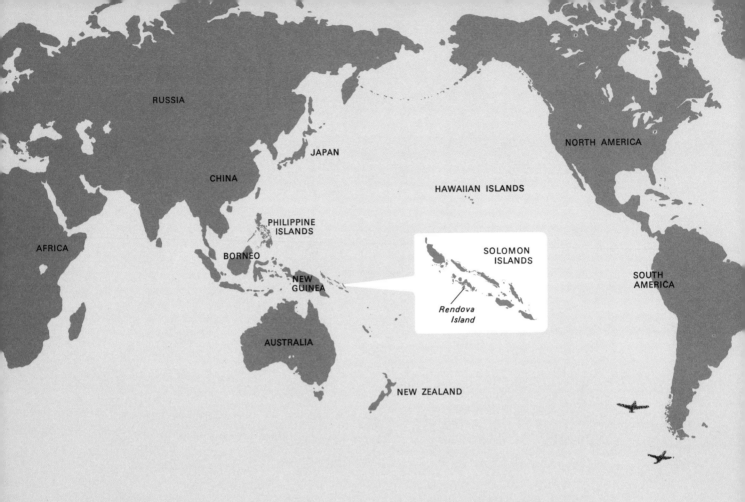

Not long after PT 109 and other boats had been transferred to a new base at Rendova, 210 miles away, enemy planes bombed the base, hoping to knock out many PT boats. The map above shows the Rendova Island area, and PT boats are shown below on maneuvers with planes.

week, Jack's craft escaped any damage from Japanese shells; then came PT 109's first real combat with Kennedy in command. A Japanese fighter plane spotted the little craft in semi-darkness and dove down for an attack, swooping across the boat with guns blazing. It dropped two bombs that missed, landing a short distance away in the water. Still, the blast rocked 109, and flying shrapnel damaged the hull and wounded two of the crewmen.

A couple of weeks later the Japanese sent a large convoy of ships through Blackett Strait. American intelligence got word of it the day before it happened. Enemy planes bombed the base at Rendova, hoping to knock out many of the PT boats, but the raid did little damage. That evening, groups of boats, including PT 109, were ordered into Blackett Strait, each with a specific assignment. Kennedy's craft was accompanied by three others with orders to patrol and keep in contact by radio. Some of the other boats were newer and contained radar sets, which made it easier for them to spot ships in the darkness, but PT 109 had to grope its way about in the inky night, depending on radio contact with the other boats to keep its bearings.

The boat crews could see flashes of fire from enemy shore batteries on a nearby island. In the darkness, the first two boats in the group became separated from PT 109 and its companion ship, PT 162. Radio communication with them was lost and Jack and the skipper of 162, Lieutenant John Lowrey, had no way of receiving orders. They cut their engines and waited for contact.

After a while they met another boat, PT 169, which had also lost contact. The three boats had changed course so many times during the night that they had no way of determining their exact position. They radioed the base at

Rendova and received instructions: Continue to look for enemy ships and when daylight comes, return to Rendova.

The three boats continued to patrol back and forth in the pitch-black night until about two-thirty in the morning. PT 109 was leading the formation, with Jack Kennedy at the wheel in the cockpit. George Ross, Jack's pal from the school in Rhode Island, had joined the crew for the mission, and was now perched up on the bow serving as lookout. The boat was idling on only one of its engines and it sliced through the dark water almost silently, the water splashing softly against the bow. As Ross peered into the inky blackness he suddenly saw a huge dark shape loom up. One of the enlisted men saw it too, and shouted "Ship at two o'clock." The ship was to the right of the bow of PT 109, toward the front.

Kennedy looked and couldn't believe his eyes. At first he thought it was another PT boat, but as the shape loomed larger and larger he realized it was a full-sized ship, heading toward them at great speed.

Ross leaped to the 37-millimeter gun on deck and grabbed frantically at a shell to load into it. Even as he did so, he knew he wouldn't have time to load and fire.

"Sound general quarters!" Kennedy yelled, and the word was passed as men sprang to their battle stations.

Jack spun the wheel to put his boat in position to fire a torpedo at the ship, but the 109, powered by only one engine, moved slowly. In seconds they realized it was too late, and that a huge ship was going to hit them head-on.

The commander of the Japanese destroyer was surprised to see the PT boat and quickly ordered a turn to ram the boat, since it was too close to fire on.

Suddenly there was a tremendous crash and the steel bow of the *Amagiri* smashed clear through the plywood PT

109, cutting it in half. Jack was thrown back from the wheel and struck a steel brace with his back. He felt a sharp pain, rolled over on the deck, and saw the giant hull a few feet away, rushing past him. The destroyer sailed on into the black night like a huge ghost.

Kennedy and most of the crew were on the forward half of the boat, which was floating. The stern, or back half, sank quickly, the weight of its engines pulling it down into the swirling sea. The engines and fuel tanks had released gasoline, which caught fire instantly. Crewmen clung precariously to the listing hull, too stunned to yell or scream. Two men, crushed by the destroyer when it hit, had been killed instantly. Others were burned as they swam in the flaming gasoline around the hull.

Jack's first thought was that there might be an explosion in the forward part of the boat any minute, and he ordered everyone off into the water. After a few minutes, when it became clear that there wouldn't be an explosion, they climbed back on. They looked in vain for the other two PT boats, hoping to be picked up, but the two crafts had left the scene, assuming that all aboard the 109 had died in the crash.

Kennedy and others who could swim splashed about in the dark water, trying to find and help the others who were injured or could not swim as well. The motor mechanic, Patrick McMahon, had been severely burned and was unable to swim much. He found himself near another crewman, Charles Harris from Boston, who shouted for help.

"Mr. Kennedy! Mr. Kennedy!" he shouted.

"I'm over here," the skipper answered. "Where are you?"

They continued to yell until Kennedy found the two men in darkness. He grasped McMahon's life vest and pulled him toward the floating hulk, which had drifted quite a distance away. Harris, who had injured his leg, struggled to swim along beside them, but he couldn't keep up.

Jack finally got McMahon safely aboard the boat, then went back to look for Harris. When he found him, Harris had become so weary that he wanted to give up. His leg was numb and he couldn't summon the strength to swim on, but after Jack helped him remove his shoes and clothing to swim better, Harris struggled on until he finally reached the remains of the 109.

Everyone was now accounted for and the weary group spent the rest of the night clinging to the hulk. They were alone in the midst of the sea, and many of the islands near them were occupied by enemy soldiers.

The evening of the Japanese attack on Rendova, groups of boats were ordered into Blackett Strait, each with a specific assignment. Kennedy's craft and three others were ordered to patrol and keep in contract by radio. During the night, a Japanese destroyer came up to Kennedy's boat suddenly and hit it head-on. There was a tremendous crash and the steel bow of the Japanese ship smashed clear through the plywood PT 109, cutting it in half (see illustration).

Survival of a Hero

As the first light of dawn crept across the silent sea, the eleven survivors atop the hulk of PT 109 could recognize the silhouettes of some of the nearby islands. They knew almost exactly where they were, but they didn't know which islands were occupied by Japanese soldiers. During the night the darkness had protected them from enemy eyes, but now they were completely exposed.

Lieutenant Jack Kennedy faced the most crucial decision he had ever had to make. He was responsible for the lives of other men and he couldn't count on help from anyone. Most of the men did not want to surrender to the enemy, but they felt certain the Japanese would find them in broad daylight. The hulk seemed to be settling in the water, and Kennedy was afraid that if they waited there all day it might sink during the night. In the darkness it would be impossible to keep all the men together, since some were weaker swimmers than others.

He decided that if they were not spotted by a search party by late afternoon, they would have to swim to one of the islands in the distance. The problem was, which one? It had to be large enough to conceal all of them, yet not so large that it would be likely to have Japanese soldiers stationed on it.

Kennedy finally chose Plum Pudding Island, even though it was farther away than some others. It seemed about the right size, and was only two or three miles from the paths the PT boats often took on their night missions. They might be able to swim out that night and signal one of them.

During the night the darkness had protected the eleven survivors of PT 109 from enemy eyes, but as the first light of dawn crept across the sea, they were completely exposed. Lieutenant Jack Kennedy decided that if they were not spotted by a search party by late afternoon, they would have to swim to one of the islands in the distance. He chose Plum Pudding Island, and after swimming nearly four hours (below) the group finally reached the island.

46

Some of the men were afraid they wouldn't be able to make the three-and-a-half mile swim to Plum Pudding. McMahon, the burned motor mechanic, was helpless. Kennedy found a large floating plank and told the men to hang onto it and push it along. They tied their shoes to the plank and secured the ship's battery-powered electric lantern to a life vest, then tied that, too. By staying together with the plank, the weaker swimmers could keep up with the stronger ones, even though it meant a frustratingly slow pace.

McMahon, however, was too weak to hold onto the plank or to swim. Kennedy decided the only chance for McMahon was for him to tow the injured sailor, whose life vest had a three-foot long strap attached to the back near the top. Kennedy seized the end of the strap in his teeth and began a breast stroke, towing McMahon along behind him.

The distance ahead was discouraging, and many swimmers would have given up in exhaustion. But Jack was determined to make it, and now his competitive spirit paid off. He hurled every bit of his strength into the long, exhausting swim. On and on he swam, pausing every now and then to rest while treading water. His jaws ached from biting into the strap, his arms and legs seemed like lead, and his injured back hurt. At times he nearly lost consciousness but he continued the grim struggle.

Finally, as the sun dipped toward the horizon nearly four hours later, Kennedy and McMahon drifted onto a white sand beach on Plum Pudding Island. Jack lay panting, unable to move any farther. Swimming with the strap in his mouth, he had swallowed a large amount of salt water, and now he was sick. Neither man could stand, and they both crawled slowly up the beach to the shelter of some bushes. Before long the other survivors struggled onto the beach with their plank. They all sat in silence, staring across the water and resting.

Suddenly the sound of an approaching boat startled them. The men dove for the bushes and lay on their stomachs, watching. A motorized Japanese barge came chugging around the bend in the island, only a couple of hundred

yards away. There were three or four armed soldiers in it. The men wondered whether the Japanese had seen them on the beach and were coming after them. Tension gripped them as the barge slowly passed by the island. Then it continued on toward a Japanese military post on another island, four miles away. They could breathe easily again, but they spoke to each other in whispers, for there might be enemy troops on the other side of their little island. If the barge had passed a few minutes earlier they would have been spotted in the water.

Jack's good judgment and heroic effort had helped them out of their dangerous situation at sea, but now the survivors had to get back to American hands safely. They had no means of traveling the forty-odd miles to the PT boat base at Rendova, and the Japanese might discover them at any time.

Jack decided to swim out into Ferguson Passage, where the PT boats often passed at night, to try to intercept one by using the battery-powered lantern. The other two officers, Ross and Thom, thought it would be suicidal, but Kennedy insisted.

At dusk he slipped into the warm tropical water, wearing only shorts, shoes, a life belt around his waist, and a 38-caliber revolver hanging from his neck on a string. The lantern was tied to a floating life vest which he pushed ahead of him on the surface. He planned to walk on the reef that surrounded the islands when possible, and to swim from the farthest point of the reef.

Soon it was pitch dark and he groped his way along the sharp coral reef, getting farther and farther away from the island. Occasionally, fish darted away from where he stepped, and he wondered if he would be attacked by sharks. It was a silent, moonless night and only the quiet sound of his movements in the water broke the stillness. He finally began to swim to the center of the passage. After he arrived, he treaded water for a long time, the lifebelt giving him some buoyancy. He waited for hours, but no boats broke the silence of his lonely vigil. He had no way of knowing that the PT boats had been sent to another area that night and would not come through Ferguson Passage.

After a long, exhausting swim back toward Plum Pudding Island in the eerie darkness, Jack began to see light in the sky. Soon it was dawn, and he discovered he was still a considerable distance from the men. He knew he didn't have the strength to make it all the way back, and when he spotted a tiny island with only one tree and some bushes, he crawled onto it and fell into a deep sleep.

Jack awoke and made it back to Plum Pudding by late morning. The men were overjoyed to see him stagger up the beach. Weak from lack of food, his feet cut from the sharp coral reef,

Only a few minutes after the survivors of PT 109 had reached Plum Pudding Island, the sound of an approaching boat startled them. They dove for the bushes as a motorized Japanese barge carrying armed soldiers (left) chugged around the bend in the island, only a couple of hundred yards away. If the barge had passed a few minutes earlier, the men would have been spotted in the water.

his hair matted, and growing a scraggly beard, he was a pitiable sight. He promptly fell into deep slumber for the rest of the day.

That night, Ensign Ross tried the same trip to intercept a PT boat, but again none came into the area. The next day Jack decided they had to move to a larger island a mile and three-quarters away, before they became too weak from lack of food. They had found only three coconuts on Plum Pudding. The other island, Olasana, had plenty of coconut palm trees, and Jack decided to take the risk that the island would not be occupied by Japanese troops.

The men used the plank again and Jack towed the injured McMahon to Olasana in another long, tiring swim. The exhausted crew slept fitfully that night, worried that there might be Japanese soldiers hidden by the trees on the island.

The next day there was still no sign of American planes or boats and the men were discouraged. Kennedy decided to swim with Ross to another island, Naru, a half mile away. They discovered a native canoe and a crate of Japanese hard candy that had been washed ashore from a wrecked ship. Kennedy, with the candy, paddled the canoe back to the men on Olasana while Ross waited on Naru.

When he arrived, he discovered that two native island men had paddled a canoe to Olasana and had met the stranded American sailors. The dark-skinned natives were loyal to the British and Americans and wanted to help them. They could paddle their way around the islands without being bothered by the Japanese, who thought them harmless. Furthermore, they knew where an Australian coast watcher was hiding on a nearby island with a radio set. His job was to spy on the Japanese in the area and report lost planes and boats to the American, British, and Australian military headquarters. He had been looking for the crew of PT 109 for several days since receiving a message from the base at Rendova that it was missing in action. The natives spoke no English, however, and could not make Kennedy understand about the coast watcher.

Jack decided to send a message all the way to Rendova. On a piece of coconut shell he carved this message to the base commander:

NATIVE KNOWS POSIT
HE CAN PILOT   11 ALIVE
NEED SMALL BOAT
      KENNEDY

Pointing in the direction of Rendova, Jack made the two natives understand that they should paddle their canoe there and deliver the coconut shell with the message. The men set off on the long trip, but stopped on an island to tell another native scout about the crew of PT 109. This scout quickly dispatched a messenger to the Australian coast watcher, Lieutenant Arthur R. Evans, to tell him where Kennedy and his men were.

Evans sent a message by radio to the base at Rendova and sent seven scouts in canoes loaded with food to Kennedy's group. When the canoes arrived, the famished men had a feast,

for the Australian had sent cans of roast beef hash, boiled fish, potatoes, yams, rice, and even cigarettes. He also had sent kerosene burners on which to cook the food, and they had their first hot meal in a week.

Evans had sent a message to Kennedy advising him to return with the natives in a canoe to the coast watcher's hiding place. There he could be in direct radio contact with Rendova. Jack lay down in the bottom of a canoe and the natives covered him with palm fronds and began paddling. Along the way, two Japanese planes swooped in and circled low over the canoe. Since they saw only the natives, they flew on.

Back at Rendova, plans were made to dispatch three PT boats to Olasana to rescue the men. When Jack reached the coast watcher's base of operations it was suggested that he have the natives paddle him all the way to the PT base without waiting for the boats to rescue his men. He refused and sent a radio message telling the PT boats to pick him up on the way to Olasana. He felt responsible for his men and wanted to lead the PT boats through the darkness to the spot where they were. Besides, he knew the island better than anyone on the PT boats.

Everything went according to plan that night and after picking up Kennedy, the PT boats collected the other ten members of the group. Soon the relieved, tired survivors were back at the base in Rendova. Jack Kennedy had faced up to the greatest challenge of his life and had performed with courage and extraordinary determination.

After Jack Kennedy and another man had swum out on two consecutive nights to try—unsuccessfully— to intercept a PT boat on patrol, Jack decided they would have to move to another island where there was food. They went to Olasana the next day, and later two native island men met the stranded sailors. The natives knew of an Australian coast watcher on a nearby island, and brought him a message Kennedy had carved on a coconut shell. The coast watcher radioed for help for the men (above), and rescue plans were put into effect from the PT base at Rendova.

Up the Washington Ladder

John F. Kennedy was promoted to full lieutenant after recuperating in "sick bay" following the rescue. He was also awarded the Navy and Marine Corps Medal for his gallantry in helping to save his crew, and the Purple Heart for the severe back injury he sustained when thrown against the steel brace of the cockpit when the 109 was struck.

Instead of requesting to be shipped back to the United States, he took command of another PT boat and took part in more combat missions before his tour of duty in the Pacific ended. On one important mission his boat came roaring in to shore to rescue nearly fifty marines who had been trapped by a larger enemy force in fierce fighting.

It finally became apparent that Kennedy had sustained permanent injuries and he was ordered back to the United States. His back, which had never been strong after his football injury at Harvard, had been permanently damaged in PT 109. His adrenal glands suffered lasting damage from the tremendous strain of swimming, and he had malaria.

His weight dropped to 125 pounds and his complexion was an unhealthy yellow.

After six months of duty as a PT boat instructor at Miami, Florida, Jack entered Chelsea Naval Hospital near Boston for treatment and tests on his back. During his stay there he visited his family at Hyannis Port on weekends. They all enjoyed Joe's cheerful letters from England, where he was piloting a Liberator bomber on anti-submarine patrols. Though he had flown the number of combat missions required to transfer to noncombat duty, he asked to remain on combat duty.

One afternoon in August of 1944, Jack was visiting his parents when word arrived that Joe was missing in action. He had volunteered to fly a special, hazardous mission against German rocket sites with a plane loaded with explosives. His bomber had suddenly blown up over the English coast and his body had not been found. The tragedy dealt the family a staggering blow. Joe had been the bright hope of the future, the proud eldest son who seemed to be headed for certain success. His father had already been thinking

---

In August of 1944, when Jack Kennedy was in a hospital near Boston for treatment of the injuries he had sustained in the PT boat collision, the Kennedy family received word that Joe was missing in action. While he had been piloting a Liberator bomber (like the ones on page 52) on a mission against German rocket sites, the plane had blown up and his body had not been found.

53

about postwar election campaigns for Joe, who was a natural politician. It took a long time for the grief of his death to become easier for the family to bear.

A few months later Jack underwent surgery at Chelsea Naval Hospital to correct the damaged discs in his back. His recovery was not complete and later he was retired from the navy for medical disability. Through his father's friend William Randolph Hearst, the owner of many newspapers, Jack got a job reporting world events. He covered some important conferences involving world leaders and was fascinated with international politics and diplomacy, as he had been in college. But reporting events was not the same as being involved in them, and Jack felt restless. He resigned and found himself, at the age of twenty-eight, wondering just what to do with his life.

It was then that his maternal grandfather, "Honey Fitz," came up with an idea that changed his life. The one-time Boston mayor was eighty-two, but still spry and alert. He suggested that Jack run in the election for United States Congressman from the Eleventh District of Massachusetts. Jack's father urged him to run. He pointed out that Joe would have carried the family name into public office, but since he was gone, Jack had an opportunity to carry on in his place.

In spite of having gone through the rigors of war combat and emerging a hero, Jack was still shy and didn't consider himself a politician of any promise. He was sure he would feel apologetic asking strangers to vote for him. But he finally agreed to run, for he knew it would mean a lot to his father and grandfather for him to enter politics.

The Eleventh District of Massachusetts, partly in Boston and partly in neighboring communities, is solidly Democratic. Jack's biggest problem was to secure the Democratic nomination in the primary election; eight other candidates had the same idea. Once he had reluctantly entered the campaign, Jack's old competitive spirit returned. He threw his energy into the fight and organized an efficient campaign. He dreaded ringing doorbells and facing crowds of voters, but he forced himself to do it. The more he campaigned, the more self-confidence he gained.

Jack won the primary election easily and four months later he won over his Republican opponent and became a United States Congressman. He moved into a rented house in Washington with his sister Eunice, who was doing social work there.

Now that he was definitely in politics as a career, Jack was determined to go as far and as fast as he could. He wanted to be the best Congressman the voters in his district had ever had, and he was already planning to run for reelection when his term expired. He set up an office in Boston to handle requests by his constituents, and the word soon got around that Congressman Kennedy really cared about the voters back home.

Joe Kennedy had been the bright hope of the future, the proud eldest son who seemed to be headed for certain political success. His father had already been thinking about postwar election campaigns for Joe, who was a natural politician. In 1946, Jack's maternal grandfather, "Honey Fitz," suggested that he run in the election for United States Congressman from the Eleventh District of Massachusetts. Since Joe would have carried the family name into public office, his father was delighted at the idea that Jack would have an opportunity to carry on in his place. Jack entered the campaign reluctantly (opposite) but won over his Republican opponent and began his career in politics.

He enjoyed himself immensely in Washington and was popular with fellow Congressmen. As a bachelor Congressman, he dated many of the capital city's prettiest career girls and socialites. On weekends he flew to Palm Beach, Florida, where his parents had a winter home, or to Hyannis Port, to swim, sail, and play golf.

Jack worked hard at learning the art of politics; he studied the intricacies of party politics and strategy and practiced his public speaking style until it improved. He began giving speeches all over Massachusetts in order to make himself known statewide. During this time, he found a group of dedicated helpers who stayed with him all through his career in politics.

Kennedy won an easy victory in his reelection campaign of 1948 and again in 1950. He now began to devote more of his interest to foreign affairs. The world was still in a tense period, even though World War II had ended with complete victory for America, Great Britain, and their allies. Hitler and Mussolini were dead, their governments crushed along with their countries in the terrible war. Japan, too, had surrendered to General Douglas MacArthur when its leaders became convinced they could not win the war.

Russia had been an ally of the United States against Germany, Italy, and Japan, and had suffered greatly at the hands of invading German troops. But by the end of the war, the Russian army had been built into one of the most powerful in the world. The Russian government was not a democracy, but was composed of officials of the Communist party. A dictator, Joseph Stalin, ruled with an iron hand and the people had little chance to choose their leaders. Stalin was every bit as ruthless as Hitler had been. The goal of the Russian dictator and his fellow Communists was to force every country in the world to have a communist government, with Russia as the leader of nations. Their agents managed to take over the governments of many countries and they helped the Communists in China seize control of that huge nation in a bloody civil war.

The little country of Korea, near China and Japan, had been divided after the war. North Korea was ruled by a communist government installed by the Russians, and South Korea ruled itself with a non-communist government. The Communists believed that South Korea could be taken over by force. They knew the United States and other democracies did not want war, and they were certain that the North Korean army could conquer South Korea with no interference.

In June, 1950, the Communists invaded South Korea. But the President of the United States, Harry S. Truman, was determined that the democratic nations would not allow an aggressor to conquer a weaker nation. A painful lesson had been learned when Hitler had been allowed to bully smaller countries in Europe. This time America acted swiftly to defend the invaded country. The United Nations voted to send a collective force of troops to defend South

When Jack Kennedy became a United States Congressman, he moved to Washington, where he was popular with fellow Congressmen. Opposite: Representatives of six Massachusetts veterans organizations pose on the Capitol steps with Representative John F. Kennedy.

Korea. Most of the United Nations troops were American, and General Douglas MacArthur was placed in command of the United Nations army. The bloody war raged for more than three years and ended in a stalemate, with neither side the winner. But the Communists had been met by force and they had failed to capture South Korea. America and other democracies had proved that they would not allow more international bullying of small countries.

In 1952, General Dwight D. Eisenhower, commander of allied armies in Europe during World War II, was elected President of the United States. He was a Republican who was so popular that many other Republican candidates for Congress were elected along with him. One notable exception was in Massachusetts, where Congressman John F. Kennedy worked hard and upset veteran Senator Henry Cabot Lodge for the Senate. Lodge was popular, and Jack had been warned that it would be difficult to beat him. But the challenge spurred him on and he campaigned harder than ever before in his political career. The campaign was exhausting, but Jack refused to slow down or give up, even though Lodge was favored. On election day he won by 70,000 votes and Massachusetts had a new, young Senator. Jack's name began to be known as he made speeches in many parts of the country and helped the Democratic party raise funds.

One day before his election campaign for the Senate, Kennedy had been interviewed by a beautiful young reporter-photographer for the Washington *Times-Herald*, Jacqueline Bouvier. The daughter of a very wealthy, socially prominent family, she had taken a leave of absence from her college studies to work as the newspaper's "Inquiring Camera Girl."

Jack and Jacqueline were soon going out together often, to concerts, parties, and movies. After his hectic senatorial campaign was over they saw each other more frequently and found that they missed each other when they were apart. Jack, certain that he had found the woman he wanted to marry, proposed, and on September 12, 1953, the hand-

In 1952, Congressman Kennedy campaigned hard and upset veteran Senator Henry Cabot Lodge for the Senate. On the day before his election campaign, Kennedy had been interviewed by a beautiful young reporter–photographer, Jacqueline Bouvier (opposite). Jack and Jacqueline were soon going out together often, and after the hectic campaign was over, saw each other even more frequently.

some Senator and the beautiful society girl were married in Newport, Rhode Island.

Jacqueline, or "Jackie," as she was called, quickly fitted into the large, clannish Kennedy family. Even though the sons and daughters had grown up, the family gathered almost weekly at the home in Hyannis Port or at Palm Beach. It was a noisy, happy group; they sailed, swam, played tennis and touch football with great enthusiasm. Their small children added a gay, youthful note to the atmosphere and the grandparents, Joseph and Rose, loved every minute of it.

These should have been some of the happiest days of Jack's life, but fate held another crisis in store for him. The pain in his back became so severe that he had to use crutches all the time. Doctors couldn't agree on the best course to take. Some said a dangerous, delicate operation involving a double fusion of the spinal discs was the only chance he would have to walk normally again. Others said the operation would be too risky, since his adrenal insufficiency left him with no protection against bleeding and infection, and he might not survive. The final decision was up to Jack himself. After thinking about it, he said he would rather die than spend the rest of his life on crutches.

In October, 1954, the difficult operation was performed at a hospital in New York. After three months of painful recovery, a second operation was performed. The chances of his survival did not look good and a priest was called in to give the last rites of the Catholic church. Jackie waited and prayed through the long operation. Finally a surgeon gave her the news that the surgery had been successful. In the days that followed, she was at Jack's bedside continually.

Jack had to remain in bed for weeks. He grew restless and decided to write a book he had been thinking about for some time. It was a collection of stories about political figures who had had the courage to make good decisions that were unpopular with the public. One of his political aides, Ted Sorenson, dug up material for him in the Library of Congress and Jack worked day after day writing the manuscript. When at last it was finished, he titled it *Profiles In Courage*. Soon after it was published it became a best seller, and later was awarded the Pulitzer Prize for biography. Jack still had "the gift of a writer" in him, as his early school teacher had told him.

Even more important, he still had the will to overcome a crisis and the courage to defy death.

Jack Kennedy proposed to Jacqueline Bouvier, and on September 12, 1953, the handsome Senator and the beautiful society girl were married in Newport, Rhode Island (opposite).

Time To Move Ahead

By 1956, so many people in the Democratic party knew and liked the youthful Senator John F. Kennedy that they began to think seriously of nominating him for vice-president at the Democratic convention. Former Governor Adlai E. Stevenson of Illinois was expected to be the party's candidate for president, but there was no favorite for the vice-presidential nomination. After Stevenson was nominated, the balloting took place for vice-president. Kennedy lost by a narrow margin to Senator Estes Kefauver, but made such a good showing that most of the party delegates knew that this young Senator would be a man to reckon with in the future.

The Democrats went down to defeat against the popular President Eisenhower, and Jack was glad he hadn't been part of the losing team after all.

The loss might have been blamed on his religion, since some people in the country didn't want to vote for a Catholic candidate. They didn't understand the religion and thought a Catholic had to take orders from the church hierarchy in Rome. But by now he knew that he wanted to run for president in the next election in 1960. He felt he was qualified and he had strong feelings about how the government should be run. He wanted to be able to help his country by providing outstanding leadership, and he felt confident that the majority of the American people would vote for a president because of his ability, not his religion.

During the next three years, Kennedy made hundreds of speeches all over the country, giving his views on international problems and the vital issues at home in the United States. As the

---

Senator Kennedy lost by a narrow margin the 1956 Democratic nomination for the vice-presidency, but during the next three years he made hundreds of speeches all over the country, giving his views on international problems and the vital issues at home in the United States. He knew by then that he wanted to run for president in the 1960 election, and campaigned energetically (opposite).

time drew closer for the Democratic party nominating convention, he entered primary elections in several states. These elections give voters a chance to show which candidates they prefer for president before the political parties nominate their candidates. With the help of his aides and his brother Robert, who became his campaign manager, Jack waged the most efficient, hardworking campaign in history. He met more people, made more speeches, and appeared on television more often than a candidate ever had before. The intelligent planning and hard work paid off, for the voters became familiar with Kennedy and his views and they voted him to victory in each primary election. He was very forthright about the religious issue and explained over and over that as president his religion would not interfere with his loyalty and duty to his country.

Jack's main rival for the Democratic party's presidential nomination was the able, experienced Senator Lyndon B. Johnson of Texas. He had done a masterful job as Senate Majority Leader for several years and was respected in the government. But Kennedy's intelligence and youthful enthusiasm had caught the imagination of the public and the delegates nominated him on the first ballot. When it came time to choose the nominee for vice-president, Kennedy chose Lyndon Johnson, for he felt the experienced majority leader would not only help greatly to win the election, but would be the best-qualified man to take over the leadership of the country in the event it became necessary. The delegates nominated Johnson and the Kennedy-Johnson team began campaigning for the presidential and vice-presidential election in November, 1960.

The Republican party nominated the vice-president who had been in office under Eisenhower, Richard M. Nixon, to run for president. They chose United Nations Ambassador Henry Cabot Lodge, Jack's old rival from Boston, to run for vice-president.

Nixon was better known to most people than Kennedy was, because he had been in the public spotlight for eight years as vice-president, while Jack had been just one of a hundred senators. Kennedy's most difficult task was to convince the majority of the

---

As election time drew closer for the Democratic party nominating convention, Senator Kennedy entered primary elections in several states and waged the most efficient, hardworking campaign in history. At the convention, he was nominated on the first ballot. He is shown here (opposite bottom) as he gives a speech to the nominating convention in Los Angeles and in a campaign parade (opposite top) as election time nears.

"...this is a great country but I think
it could be a greater country
... I think it's time
America started moving again."

public that he was a well-qualified statesman and had more ability than Nixon, who had more experience in a top job. He did this beautifully in a series of four debates on nationwide television. The two candidates discussed the major problems confronting America and the world, and gave their opinions on how to approach these problems.

Nixon's main argument was that the eight years of Republican administration had brought stable leadership and prosperity; people should vote for him to continue this leadership. He had been second in line under President Eisenhower and knew the problems of running the executive branch of the government, and how to deal with them. He cited statistics to show that Americans were better off than they had ever been before.

Kennedy's argument was that American leadership had grown stale, and that the same old thinking was used on new, complex problems. It was true that many Americans were better off

economically than ever before, but there were many others who were not, he pointed out. Certain areas of the country were poverty-stricken. He felt that a special effort should be made by the government to abolish this poverty in the midst of the nation's general prosperity. He also argued that America was standing still, not moving ahead economically and socially. The productivity of the country was not increasing fast enough, and there was still much discrimination against Negroes and other minority groups. Kennedy felt it was time for the government to step in and make stronger laws to guarantee equal rights for all Americans, regardless of race. He also felt that America needed more-dynamic leadership in its foreign relations, to improve its prestige around the world.

"I am not satisfied ... with the progress we are making . . . but this is a great country but I think it could be a greater country . . . I think it's time America started moving again," he declared during the television debates.

Kennedy's running mate in the 1960 election campaign was Lyndon Johnson, senator from Texas (shown opposite, top, with Kennedy). The Republican opposition were Richard Nixon, candidate for the presidency, and Henry Cabot Lodge, candidate for the vice-presidency. In the picture at the bottom of page 66 are, left to right, Nixon, Mrs. Lodge, Mrs. Nixon, and Lodge.

In November, 1960, the American public elected John F. Kennedy President of the United States. It was the closest election anyone could remember, but he had won, and immediately began to prepare for the presidency. He is shown at left with his brother Bobby, who was his campaign manager and, later, Attorney General.

The young Senator's idealism appealed especially to younger voters. He was not content to let things stand, but wanted to strive toward the goal, or ideal, of a better America for everybody. His intelligent, factual statements convinced many people that he was a well-informed statesman with the ability to lead the country.

The television debates benefited Kennedy more than they did Nixon. They gave the public a chance to see the two candidates together, and they showed that Kennedy was not an inexperienced candidate but compared favorably as a mature statesman. Kennedy's wit and charm appealed to many voters and he always took the initiative with fresh ideas.

Jack continued his same arguments throughout the long, exhausting campaign. On election day in November, the American public seemed equally divided in favor of the two candidates and throughout the long evening as the vote totals were reported, the outcome was in doubt. Jack waited with his family and close political friends at the family home in Hyannis Port, watching the returns on television. Long after midnight the result was still in doubt, although Jack was leading. He finally decided to go to bed and wait for the results in the morning, and he persuaded most of the group to do the same. Only his brother Robert sat up all night, studying the vote totals as they came in.

The great moment arrived in the morning when Nixon conceded that he had lost, and John F. Kennedy was the newly elected President of the United States. It was the closest election that anyone could remember—he had won by less than 120,000 of the 69 million votes cast. But however close, he had won, and now he began to prepare for the presidency. It was the happiest moment of Joseph P. Kennedy's life; the other members of the family, including Jackie, were equally elated. But Jack wasted little time celebrating. He was already thinking ahead to the greatest of all the challenges he had ever faced.

Triumph and Tragedy

John F. Kennedy's first task after being elected president was to select a cabinet of well-qualified men. For Secretary of Defense he chose Robert McNamara, president of Ford Motor Company, a brilliant man and an efficient organizer. He picked a distinguished, experienced State Department official, Dean Rusk, as Secretary of State, and the other Cabinet jobs were filled by equally capable men. When it came time to choose the Attorney General of the United States, he could think of no one better qualified than his own brother Robert, a lawyer and an intelligent organizer.

Kennedy had no difficulty in finding well-qualified young volunteers for positions in all branches of the government. His administration, called the "New Frontier," attracted enthusiastic young people who wanted to play a part in government by this new generation. The President himself, and his lovely young wife, symbolized the youth and freshness of America's new leaders from the day of the Inauguration in 1961. They had two children, a little girl named Caroline and a boy named John F. Kennedy, Jr. The White House echoed with the gaiety of youth as it had not done in years.

America had often been criticized by older nations as lacking in culture and it had been said that the country's leaders reflected this lack. The Kennedys set out to change that image by setting an example for everyone. A new elegance was seen in White House dinners and parties, with the handsome President and his wife setting the style. Learning and culture were prized and encouraged, and the nation's leading writers, artists, scientists, musicians, and intellectuals were often invited to the White House. Cultural programs and entertainment by ballet troupes, opera stars, and actors were common. Americans read about these events with pride in their country's culture.

President and Mrs. Kennedy symbolized the youth and freshness of America's new leaders from the day of the inauguration in 1961. They had two children, and the White House echoed with the gaiety of youth as it had not done in years. The President and his wife Jacqueline are shown opposite as they leave the White House for the Inaugural Ball.

"... This country cannot afford to be materially rich and spiritually poor ..."

"The quality of American life must keep pace with the quantity of American goods," the President said. "This country cannot afford to be materially rich and spiritually poor."

Kennedy's fervent idealism continued to attract young people. He created the Peace Corps, a group of volunteer workers who went to live in poor, underdeveloped countries and helped build roads and educate the citizens. This gave young Americans, who had grown up with many material comforts, an opportunity to give of themselves to help the less-fortunate people of the world. Peace Corps workers lived in huts and worked alongside peasants in tiny villages and farms all over the world. They taught school and showed people how to raise better crops to improve their living standards and health.

And they showed the world that Americans cared about their fellow citizens in other countries.

For John and Jacqueline Kennedy, the hectic life of political campaigning gave way to the pleasant life in the White House where they could see more of each other and their children. These were the happiest years of their marriage. Caroline and John, Jr. would often scamper around the White House and drop in to see their father when he was working in his office. He swam in the White House pool with them and walked around the grounds in good weather.

But the relaxed, pleasant life of the popular young President and his family did not lighten the grave responsibility of his job. As head of the most powerful nation in the world, he worked long hours handling various government

The Kennedy family picture on page 72 shows Caroline kissing her new baby brother, John Fitzgerald Kennedy, Jr. The picture was taken at Palm Beach, Florida.

Above, President Kennedy addresses a joint session of the 87th Congress in the House Chamber as he delivers his State of the Union address in January, 1962. Seated behind him are Vice President Lyndon Johnson and House Speaker John McCormack. Below, the President hands to Ambassador Adlai Stevenson the first pen used to sign a bill for U.S. purchase of United Nations bonds. Opposite, the President is surrounded by a large group of aides, military men, and members of the Secret Service as he walks on crutches from his jet plane to a waiting helicopter at Andrews Air Force Base in the summer of 1961. Kennedy, returning from a brief visit to Palm Beach, was suffering from the recurrent back trouble that plagued him from the time of his PT boat injury during World War II.

crises. New independent nations were emerging in Africa after long colonial rule by European countries. Russia, led by the fiery Chairman Nikita Khrushchev, was opposed to the United States and a rival for influence around the world. The communist countries continued to try to overthrow the democratic governments of other nations and trouble flared up from time to time. With massive United States aid, the countries of western Europe had recovered from the damage of World War II and were now strong, prosperous democracies. After an enlightened occupation by American forces under General Douglas MacArthur, Japan had taken its place again among nations as a prosperous democracy. But the Communist rulers of China hated the United States and caused trouble in Asia, particularly in Viet Nam, where they encouraged local Communists to seize control. America supported the non-communist government and sent aid and military advisors.

Closer to home an even graver danger lay in Cuba, an island nation only ninety miles from Florida, where a pro-Russian Communist named Fidel Castro had seized control of the government. He, too, was opposed to the United States. He accepted military aid from Russia in order to build up large armed forces and threaten other Latin American countries.

Castro had driven out many freedom-loving Cubans, who had settled in the United States as refugees. They planned to return to their home country and throw out the dictator and his Communist friends. The American government under President Eisenhower had helped them train soldiers to invade Cuba and the date was set for April,

Kennedy worked long hours handling various government crises, planning new programs such as the Peace Corps, and meeting with heads of other nations. He is shown at left with the presidents of Mali (top) and Indonesia, and opposite, bottom, with the charge d'affaires of Sierra Leone, Africa. Opposite, top: A poultry specialist in the Peace Corps who helped the people of India learn more about food production and use.

In April of 1961, many freedom-loving Cubans who had been driven out of their country by pro-Russian Communist Fidel Castro, planned to return to their home country and throw out the dictator and his Communist friends. Though the American government had helped these Cubans train soldiers, American military forces would not take part in the invasion since it was a matter involving only Cubans. Information that thousands of Cuban citizens would rise up against the communist government when the invaders landed proved to be tragically untrue, and the Bay of Pigs invasion (below) was a disastrous failure. Castro's forces spotted the freedom fighters coming ashore and soon defeated them with superior weapons and manpower.

1961. American military forces would not take part in the invasion, since this was a matter involving Cubans, but they would supply guns and ammunition. The Central Intelligence Agency informed the new President that thousands of Cuban citizens would rise up against the communist government once the invaders landed.

This proved to be tragically untrue, and Castro's forces spotted the freedom fighters coming ashore on the coast and soon defeated them with superior weapons and manpower. The brave invaders needed American help, but the Presi-dent felt the United States could not openly invade a small neighboring country. He had to sit by and watch Castro's forces win a victory, and it made him sick at heart. He would not have permitted the hopeless venture if he had not been wrongly advised by his own government experts. But, characteristically, John Kennedy refused to place the blame on anyone but himself. He did, however, quietly order an investigation of the Central Intelligence Agency to find out what went wrong so that the mistake would not be repeated in the future.

Later that year the President and Mrs. Kennedy flew to Europe where they were greeted with wild enthusiasm by crowds in France. After meetings with President Charles De Gaulle, they went on to Vienna, Austria, for an important meeting with Nikita Khrushchev, the Russian Communist ruler. Kennedy had hoped to approach the problems of Russian-American relations with new ideas, and he felt that a meeting with Khrushchev would be a good first step to take. Kennedy believed that if both countries were less rigid in their demands of one another, they might agree on a few points and get along better. A very touchy problem existed at the time of their meeting, concerning the city of Berlin, the old capital of Germany. Since the war, Germany had been split in half, with East Germany under a Russian-installed communist government and West Germany under a free democracy. But the city of Berlin, which lay inside East Germany, was also split in half and West Berlin was a free democratic society under the occupation of American, British, and French forces. The isolated city was considered part of West Germany, but the Communists did not recognize it. This part of the city was so much more prosperous than the communist part that many Germans went to West Berlin to live. The Russians had blockaded Berlin in 1949 by refusing to allow Allied trucks to drive there from West Germany, but the Allies flew in supplies for the West Berliners in a massive airlift.

Kennedy and Khrushchev had a tense meeting about Berlin, and the Russian leader insisted that West Berlin would eventually have to become part of Communist East Germany. Kennedy warned him that if the Communists tried to take it, America would defend it by force. Neither leader would give in to the other and a few months later the Communists erected a huge wall between East and West Berlin, so that no more Germans could go to live in West Berlin.

The Kennedys enjoyed a friendly tour of South America, where they were greeted with great enthusiasm. South Americans knew that here was an American president who really cared about their problems. Kennedy formed the Alliance for Progress, a program that encouraged Latin American nations to join together. Unified, they could help themselves solve their problems of poverty with help from the United States.

True to his idealism, President Kennedy fought for a better America for Negroes and other minority groups. He asked Congress to pass a Civil Rights Bill that would guarantee some of the basic rights that were being denied to Negroes. The law would protect their right to vote, which was being denied them in some states in the South. It also provided equal opportunity in jobs, public accommodations such as hotels and restaurants, and the right to attend better schools with white children. Conservative members of Congress delayed passage of the bill, but Kennedy knew that it would eventually be passed.

In October, 1962, another grave crisis confronted John F. Kennedy and it took all the judgment and wisdom at his

---

In 1961, President Kennedy met with Nikita Khrushchev, the Russian Communist ruler, in Vienna, Austria. At the time of their meeting, the East-West split of the city of Berlin, the old capital of Germany, was a touchy problem. West Berlin was a free democratic society that lay inside Communist East Germany. When Khrushchev insisted that it would have to become a part of East Germany, Kennedy warned that if the Communists tried to take it America would defend it by force. Shortly afterward, the Communists erected a huge wall between East and West Berlin, so that no more East Germans could go to live in West Berlin. In the picture on page 80, a defecting East Berlin soldier leaps over a barbed wire barricade to escape into West Berlin.

command to prevent the world from being plunged into a terrible war. Fidel Castro had allowed Russian forces to enter Cuba and set up ballistic missile bases aimed at the United States. Both the Russians and Cubans lied to the world by announcing that there were no intermediate-range missiles in Cuba capable of hitting the United States. But American planes flying over Cuba on intelligence missions took aerial photographs of the missiles, and it was proved that the Russians indeed had them aimed at the United States and were constructing more bases.

The security of the country was at stake. America could not allow the Communists to keep the missile bases. Kennedy realized he would have to demand that the Russians remove the missiles. But if they refused, it could mean the start of a war with atomic weapons. Both America and Russia had enough atomic missiles to destroy each other and the rest of the world.

The lights in the White House burned late at night as the President met with Vice-President Johnson, Defense Secretary McNamara, Attorney General Robert Kennedy, and other aides. They drew up a plan to remove the missile threat from Cuba, hoping the result would not mean war with Russia. The United States Navy was instructed to form a blockade around Cuba to prevent ships from bringing in any more missiles. If this failed, an army was standing by in Florida to invade Cuba and occupy the country. The problem was, what would the Russians do when their ships reached the American blockade? Would war break out? Would the world be blown up in a nuclear holocaust?

Kennedy appeared on nationwide television the next evening and told the

---

In October of 1962, American U2 planes (like the one above) flew over Cuba on intelligence missions and took aerial photographs (opposite top) of intermediate-range missiles aimed at the United States. Russia and Cuba had both previously denied that there were such missiles in Cuba. The security of the United States was at stake, and President Kennedy and his aides immediately drew up a plan to remove the missile threat from Cuba, hoping the result would not mean war with Russia. The United States Navy formed a blockade around Cuba to prevent ships from bringing in any more missiles. In the picture at the bottom of page 83, a United States destroyer checks the cargo of a Soviet freighter.

MISSILE TRANSPORTERS

12 PROB GUIDELINES MISSILES

HEAVY EQUIPMENT

5 MISSILE DOLLIES

20 LONG CYLINDRICAL TANKS

MISSILE TRANSPORTERS

OPEN STORAGE

American people about the action he had taken. The world held its breath and waited as several Russian ships continued on their way toward Cuba across the Atlantic Ocean. But at last they stopped and one of them was intercepted by American ships and searched for missiles. The Russians did nothing; Kennedy knew he had won a war of nerves.

He followed up by demanding that the Russians remove the missiles already in Cuba and ship them back to Russia. When Khrushchev quickly agreed, it became clear that the Russian leaders were as horrified by the prospect of nuclear war as were the other people of the world. The missiles were soon shipped back to Russia.

President Kennedy had led the country through a very dangerous period with calm determination, and his reputation as a great leader grew enormously —not only in the United States but throughout the world. He felt more confident than at any other time since he had taken the oath as president. Halfway through his first term, he began to think about the many more things he would be able to accomplish after being reelected to a second term. There was little doubt that he would win the next election by a wide margin. As the youngest man ever elected president, he looked forward to retiring after two terms while only in his early fifties, and devoting his later years to helping his country in other ways.

The President appeared on television (left) and told the American people about the action he had taken. When the Russians did nothing about their ships being searched for missiles, Kennedy knew he had won a war of nerves and followed up by demanding that the Russians remove the missiles already in Cuba and ship them back to Russia. Khrushchev (opposite) quickly agreed and the missiles were soon shipped out of Cuba.

In November, 1963, the President and Mrs. Kennedy made a tour of several Texas cities and were greeted by friendly crowds. One of the last stops on their tour was Dallas, where the President was to make a speech at a luncheon. After landing at the airport in the presidential plane, "Air Force One," the Kennedys began a ten-mile tour through Dallas in the open-convertible presidential limousine. With them were Texas Governor John Connally and his wife. Vice-President and Mrs. Lyndon Johnson were in another car in the motorcade, which wound slowly through the streets. The crowds of people greeted the President warmly, and he was pleased at the friendly reception.

Waving and smiling, he was borne along at a slow speed until the car passed a six-story building called the Texas School Book Depository. Suddenly shots rang out and the President slumped into Mrs. Kennedy's arms, blood spilling from his head. Governor Connally, hit by a bullet in the chest, also slumped down.

An agent leaped onto the back of the car to protect the President as pandemonium broke loose and the car sped forward. The driver headed at high speed for a large hospital as the shocked police and citizens wondered just what had happened. At the hospital, attendants quickly rushed the President to an emergency room, where doctors worked frantically to save his life. It was too late. At the age of forty-six, John F. Kennedy's remarkable life ended; the nation had lost its president.

Police arrested a twenty-four-year-old man named Lee Harvey Oswald, and a special government commission concluded after investigation that he had shot the President from the window of the Texas School Book Depository. A mixed-up misfit who sympathized with communism and had lived in Russia,

President and Mrs. Kennedy made a tour of several Texas cities in November, 1963, and were greeted by friendly crowds (right). In Dallas, as the Kennedy's drove through the city in a motorcade, shots suddenly rang out. The President had been killed.

Oswald didn't confess to the crime. Two days later he was killed by an enraged bystander while being taken from jail.

An hour and a half after John Kennedy's death, Lyndon B. Johnson was sworn in as president on board Air Force One in Dallas. The shocked and grief-stricken Jacqueline Kennedy stood beside him as he took the oath. The new President promised later to continue the late President's programs and work toward the goals that he would have accomplished had he lived.

The whole world was shocked at John F. Kennedy's death. Seldom, if ever, had an American president been so respected and well liked in foreign countries. People wept in the streets in many cities around the world. Americans were stunned and grief-stricken, and it seemed to most people that they had lost a close friend in the young, engaging President.

The dead President's body lay in state in the great rotunda of the Capitol Building in Washington as thousands of Americans of all ages, races and religions stood in line for hours to pay their respects. All night long they came; sometimes the line was three miles long.

Heads of countries from all over the world came to attend the funeral. The American people watched the services on television as the procession moved slowly through the streets, across the bridge to Arlington National Cemetery. Millions of people, weeping themselves, admired the courage of Jacqueline Kennedy as she marched behind her husband's coffin, determined to remain composed as she fought to control her grief. The graveside services, on a grassy hill near the city of Washington, were short. A sad sounding of taps, a rifle volley in tribute, and the world had said its farewell to a great leader.

But John Fitzgerald Kennedy had left a legacy of hope, enthusiasm, and idealism that would last as long as men believe in their fellow human beings. His belief in principles, his willingness to struggle against great odds, his hope for a better world for all people, inspired a generation—not only of grateful Americans, but of citizens of the world.

Americans were stunned and grief-stricken at the death of the young President. Heads of countries from all over the world came to attend the funeral and the American people watched the services on television as the procession (opposite) moved slowly through the streets to Arlington National Cemetery. The world said its farewell to a great leader with a sad sounding of taps and a rifle volley in tribute.

Summary

From his heroic action in war to his televised appearances as President of the United States, John F. Kennedy set standards of excellence for himself and for all Americans. He never took the easy way out and he hated indifference to challenges.

Even more importantly, he had the rare ability to transmit these attitudes to other people and to inspire citizens everywhere. His New Frontier administration was rededicated to early American ideals. He offered hope in an age of doubt, and faith that goals could be accomplished.

His own pursuit of excellence carried him over such obstacles as ill health, proximity to death, and predictions of experts that he could not succeed.

History will judge John F. Kennedy's brief presidency by more than its acts of record. It was his destiny to change the thinking of a whole generation, to give people confidence in the future, and to set an example for future generations to emulate. The effect of his life on the future of his country will be measured in centuries to come.

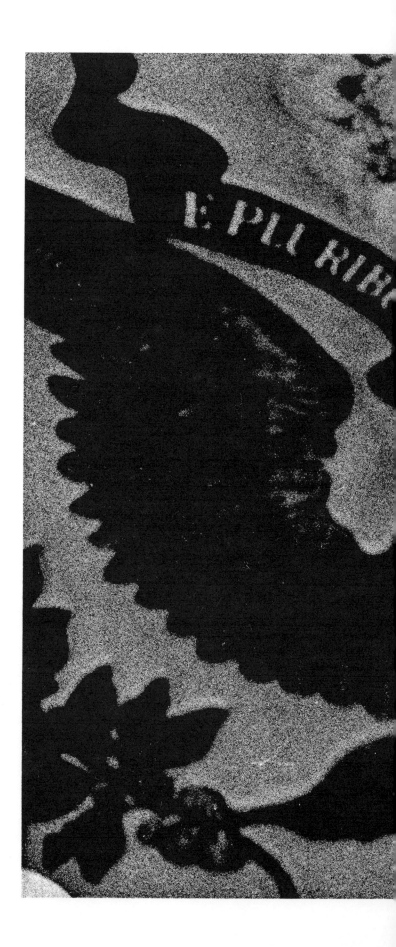

Bibliography

ADLER, BILL, ed. *John F. Kennedy and the Young People of America.* New York: McKay, 1965.

———. *The Kennedy Wit.* New York: Citadel Press, 1964.

———. *The Common Sense of Three First Ladies.* New York: Citadel Press, 1966.

———. *More Kennedy Wit.* New York: Citadel Press, 1965.

AGRONSKY, MARTIN, ed. *Let Us Begin, the first 100 days.* New York: Simon and Schuster, 1961.

ASSOCIATED PRESS. *The Torch Is Passed, the story of the death of a President.* New York: 1963.

BALLOT, PAUL, ed. *The Thousand Days.* New York: Citadel Press, 1964.

BEKESSY, JEAN (psued. Hans Habe). *The Wounded Land.* New York: Coward-McCann, 1964.

BELLI, MELVIN. *Dallas Justice.* New York: McKay, 1964.

BERGQUIST, LAURA. *A Very Special President.* New York: McGraw-Hill, 1965.

BERRY, WENDELL. *November twenty-six nineteen hundred sixty three; poem.* New York: Braziller, 1964.

BINKLEY, WILFRED. *The Man in The White House.* Baltimore: Johns Hopkins Press, 1959.

BISHOP, JIM. *A Day In The Life Of President Kennedy.* New York: Random House, 1964.

BRADLEE, BENJAMIN. *That Special Grace.* Philadelphia: Lippincott, 1964.

BROGAN, D. W. *Politics in America.* New York: Harper, 1954.

BUCHANAN, THOMAS. *Who Killed Kennedy?* New York: G. P. Putnam's Sons, 1964.

BURNS, JAMES MACGREGOR. *John Kennedy, A Political Profile.* New York: Harcourt, 1961.

CHASE, HAROLD and ALLEN LERMAN, ed. *Kennedy and the Press.* New York: Crowell, 1965.

CROWN, JAMES TRACY. *Kennedy in Power.* New York: Ballantine, 1961.

CURLEY, J. M. *I'd Do It Again.* Englewood Cliffs, New Jersey: Prentice-Hall, 1957.

CUTLER, JOHN HENRY. *"Honey Fitz": Three Steps To The White House.* New York: Bobbs-Merrill, 1962.

DANIEL, JAMES and JOHN HUBBEL. *Strike in the West: The Complete Story of the Cuban Crisis.* New York: Holt, Rinehart & Winston, 1963.

DEARBORN, NATHANIEL. *Boston Notions.* Boston, 1848.

DINNEEN, J. F. *The Purple Shamrock.* New York: W. W. Norton, 1949.

DINNEEN, JOSEPH. *The Kennedy Family.* Boston: Little, Brown & Co., 1959.

DONOVAN, ROBERT. *PT 109.* New York: McGraw-Hill, 1961.

ELLIS, G. E. *Bacon's Dictionary of Boston.* Boston: Houghton Mifflin, 1886.

EPSTEIN, EDWARD J. *Inquest.* New York: Viking Press, 1966.

FAY, PAUL BURGESS. *The Pleasure of His Company.* New York: Harper, 1966.

FINE, WILLIAM, ed. *That Day With God.* New York: McGraw-Hill, 1965.

FORD, GERALD. *Portrait of the Assassin.* New York: Simon and Schuster, 1965.

FULLER, HELEN. *Year of Trial, Kennedy's Crucial Decision.* New York: Harcourt, Brace & World, 1962.

GARDNER, GERALD, ed. *The Quotable Mr. Kennedy.* New York: Abelard-Schuman, 1962.

GARDNER, JOHN, ed. *To Turn The Tide.* New York: Harper, 1962.

GEER, CANDY. *Six White Horses; an illustrated poem about John-John.* Ann Arbor: Quill, 1964.

GLIKES, ERWIN A., ed. *Of poetry & power; poems occasioned by the Presidency and by the death of John F. Kennedy.* New York: Basic Books, 1964.

GOLDEN, H. *Mr. Kennedy and the Negroes.* Cleveland: World, 1964.

GOLDMAN, ALEX. *The Quotable Kennedy.* New York: Citadel Press, 1965.

GOLDWIN, ROBERT, ed. *Why Foreign Aid?* Chicago: Rand McNally, 1963.

GREENBERG, BRADLEY. *The Kennedy Assassination.* Stanford: Stanford University Press, 1965.

HALL, GORDON and ANN PINCHOT. *Jacqueline Kennedy.* New York: Fell, 1964.

HANDLIN, OSCAR. *Boston's Immigrants, 1790–1880.* Cambridge, Mass.: Harvard University Press, 1959.

———. *The Uprooted.* Boston: Little, Brown & Co., 1951.

HANSEN, M. L. *The Atlantic Migration.* Cambridge: Harvard University Press, 1940.

HENNESSEY, M. E. *Twenty-five Years of Massachusetts Politics.* Boston: Practical Politics, Inc., 1917.

HERSEY, JOHN. *"Survival." The New Yorker.* June 17, 1944.

HUTCHMACHER, J. *Henry Cabot Lodge.* New York: Alfred A. Knopf, 1953.

JOESTEN, JOACHIM. *Oswald: Assassin or Fall Guy?* New York: Maryani, 1964.

KAZAN, MOLLY THACHER. *Kennedy; poem.* New York: Stein, 1963.

KENNEDY, JOHN F. *A Nation of Immigrants.* New York: Harper, 1964.

———. *America The Beautiful.* Wisconsin: Country Beautiful Foundation, 1964.

KENNEDY, JOHN F. *As We Remember Joe.* Cambridge, Mass.: Harvard University Press, 1945.

———— and others. *Creative America.* New York: Ridge, 1962.

————. *Moral Crisis, The Case For Civil Rights.* Minneapolis: Gilbert, 1964.

————. *Profiles in Courage.* New York: Watts, 1964.

————. *Public Papers of the Presidents of the U.S.* Washington: National Archives & Record Service, 1958.

————. *The Burden and the Glory.* New York: Harper & Row, 1964.

————. *The Faith of J.F.K.* New York: Dutton, 1965.

————. *The Strategy of Peace.* New York: Harper, 1960.

————. *Why England Slept.* New York: Funk, 1961.

KENNEDY, JOSEPH P. *I'm For Roosevelt.* New York: Reynal & Hitchcock, 1936.

————, ed. *The Story of the Films.* Chicago: A. W. Shaw Co., 1927.

KLUCKHORN, FRANK. *America: Listen!* Darby: Monarch, 1962.

KRAUS, SIDNEY, ed. *The Great T.V. Debates.* Indiana: Indiana University Press, 1962.

LANE, MARK. *Rush To Judgment.* New York: Holt, Rinehart & Winston, 1966.

LANE, THOMAS A. *The Leadership of President Kennedy.* Caldwell, Idaho: Caxton Printers, 1964.

LASKY, VICTOR. *J.F.K.: The Man & The Myth.* New York: MacMillan, 1963.

————. *John F. Kennedy; what's behind the image.* Washington: Free World, 1960.

LIEBERSON, GODDARD, ed. *John F. Kennedy As We Remember Him.* New York: Atheneum, 1965.

LIFE. *John F. Kennedy Memorial Edition.* Chicago: Time, 1963.

LINCOLN, EVELYN. *My Twelve Years With John F. Kennedy.* New York: McKay, 1965.

LOWE, JACQUES. *Portrait; the emergence of John F. Kennedy.* New York: McGraw-Hill, 1961.

McCARTHY, JOE. *The Remarkable Kennedys.* New York: Dial Press, 1960.

MANCHESTER, WILLIAM. *Portrait of a President.* Boston: Little, Brown & Co., 1962.

MARKMANN, CHARLES. *John F. Kennedy.* New York: St. Martins, 1961.

MARTIN, RALPH. *Front Runner, Dark Horse.* New York: Doubleday, 1960.

MAZO, EARL. *Richard Nixon.* New York: Harper, 1959.

MEAGHER, SYLVIA. *Subject Index to the Warren Report.* New York: Scarecrow Press, 1966.

MEYERSON, MAXWELL. *Memorable Quotations of John F. Kennedy.* New York: Crowell, 1965.

NATIONAL BROADCASTING CO. *Seventy Hours and Thirty Minutes.* New York: Random House, 1966.

NIXON, RICHARD. *Six Crises.* New York: Doubleday, 1962.

NEW YORK TIMES. *The Kennedy Years.* New York: Viking, 1964.

O'HARA, WILLIAM, ed. *John F. Kennedy on Education.* New York: Columbia Teachers College Press, 1965.

OPOTOWSKY, STAN. *The Kennedy Government.* New York: Popular Library, 1961.

PIKE, JAMES A. *A Roman Catholic In The White House.* New York: Doubleday, 1960.

ROSSITER, W. S., ed. *Days and Ways in Old Boston.* Boston: R. H. Stearns, 1915.

ROWEN, HERBERT. *The Free Enterprisers.* New York: G. P. Putnam's Sons, 1964.

SALINGER, PIERRE, ed. *A Tribute To John F. Kennedy.* Chicago: Encyclopedia Britannica, 1964.

————. *With Kennedy.* New York: Doubleday, 1966.

SAUNDERS, DORIS, ed. *The Kennedy Years and the Negro.* Chicago: Johnson, 1964.

SAUVAGE, LEO. *The Oswald Affair.* Cleveland: World, 1966.

SCHLESINGER, ARTHUR. *A Thousand Days.* Boston: Houghton, 1965.

————. *Kennedy or Nixon?* New York: Macmillan, 1960.

SCHNEIDER, NICHOLAS, ed. *Religious Views of President John F. Kennedy.* St. Louis: Herder, 1965.

SCHOOR, GENE. *Young John Kennedy.* New York: Harcourt, Brace & World, Inc., 1963.

SETTEL, T. S., ed. *The Faith of J.F.K.* New York: Dutton, 1965.

SEVAREID, ERIC, ed. *Candidates 1960.* New York: Basic Books, 1959.

SHAW, MARK. *The John F. Kennedys.* Toronto: Ambassador, 1964.

SHAW, MAUD. *White House Nannie.* New York: New American Library, 1966.

SHEPARD, TAYEWELL. *John F. Kennedy, man of the sea.* New York: Morrow, 1965.

SIDNEY, HUGH. *John F. Kennedy, President.* New York: Atheneum, 1964.

SORENSON, THEODORE. *Kennedy.* New York: Harper, 1965.

SZULC, TAD and KARL MYER. *The Cuban Invasion.* New York: Ballantine, 1962.

TANZER, LESTER, ed. *The Kennedy Circle.* Washington: Luce, 1961.

THAYER, MARY. *Jacqueline Bouvier Kennedy.* New York: Doubleday, 1961.

The Life and Words of John F. Kennedy. Elm Grove, Wisconsin: Country Beautiful Foundation.

TIPTON, HAROLD. *One Liberal's Answer: Nix On Kennedy.* Seattle, 1960.

UNITED PRESS INTERNATIONAL. *Four Days.* New York: American Heritage Publishing Co., 1964.

U.S. COMMITTEE FOR THE U.N. *Homage to a Friend.* New York: 1964.

U.S. CONGRESS. *Memorial Addresses.* Washington: U.S. Government Printing Office, 1964.

U.S. PRESIDENT'S COMMISSION ON THE ASSASSINATION OF PRESIDENT KENNEDY. "Warren Report." Washington: U.S. Government Printing Office, 1964.

WHALEN, RICHARD. *The Founding Father; the story of Joseph P. Kennedy.* New York: New American Library, 1964.

WHIPPLE, CHANDLER. *Lt. John F. Kennedy, Expendable!* New York: Envoy, 1962.

WHITE, THEODORE. *The Making of The President, 1960.* New York: Atheneum, 1961.

WICKER, THOMAS. *Kennedy Without Tears.* New York: Morrow, 1964.

WIESBERG, HAROLD. *Whitewash.* Hyattstown, Md., 1965.

WOLFENSTEIN, MARTHA. *Children and the Death of a President; multidisciplinary studies.* New York: Doubleday, 1965.

WOLFF, PERRY SIDNEY. *A Tour of the White House with Mrs. John F. Kennedy.* New York: Doubleday, 1962.

WOODHAM-SMITH, CECIL. *The Great Hunger: Ireland 1845-1849.* New York: Harper & Row, 1963.

WOODS, R. A., ed. *Americans in Process.* Boston: 1902.

Index